My Little Bible Picture Book

Is Presented To

Ishita Ghosh

On

May 27, 1993

By

Discovery Kingdom

◆

*Let the little children come to me, and do not hinder them,
for the kingdom of God belongs to such as these.*

MARK 10:14

◆ My Little Bible Picture Book ◆

Chariot Books™
David C. Cook Publishing Co.

Chariot Books is an imprint of David C. Cook Publishing Co.
David C. Cook Publishing Co., Elgin, Illinois 60120
David C. Cook Publishing Co., Weston, Ontario

MY LITTLE BIBLE PICTURE BOOK

© 1980, 1981, 1982, 1985, 1986, 1987, 1988 by David C. Cook Publishing Co.

Cover and interior design by Dawn Lauck

First Printing, 1988
Printed in Singapore
92 93 94 95 96 97   15 14 13 12 11 10 9 8

Library of Congress Cataloging-in-Publication Data
My little Bible picture book.
        p.   cm.
    Summary: Double page spreads present major Bible stories from Creation to the Apostles, with pictures, prayers, and Scripture verses.
    ISBN 1-55513-513-7
    1. Bible stories, English.   2. Bible—Illustrations—Juvenile literature.   [1. Bible stories.]
BS551.2.M9 1988
220.9'505—dc19   88-4575
                                                                                           CIP
                                                                                            AC

CONTENTS

In the Beginning
GENESIS 1:1–5

A long, long time ago, God made heaven and earth. Everything was dark—just like when you shut your eyes.

So God said, "I'll make daytime." Because God made daytime, look at all the things you can see.

PRAYER

Thank You, God, for making daytime.

A BIBLE VERSE TO REMEMBER

God saw that the light was good, and he separated the light from the darkness. GENESIS 1:4

God Made Nighttime
GENESIS 1:1–5

When God made daytime, He made nighttime, too. At night it's dark outside. What can you see in the sky at night? What do you do at night?

PRAYER
Thank You, God, for making
nighttime dark so I can sleep.

A BIBLE VERSE TO REMEMBER
God called the light "day," and the darkness he called "night."
And there was evening, and there was morning—the first day.

GENESIS 1:5

God Made Water and Land
GENESIS 1:6–13

God made the land for us to live on. Some land is flat. And some land is hilly. He made all the plants that grow on the land.

God made water, too. He made little streams and big oceans. Plants and animals and people all need water to live.

PRAYER
Thank You, God, for hills to climb
and water to drink.

A BIBLE VERSE TO REMEMBER

God called the dry ground "land," and the gathered waters he called "seas." And God saw that it was good. **GENESIS 1:10**

God Made Water Animals
GENESIS 1:20–23

God made some special animals that live in the water. What are they called? Fish!

What other water animals do you see in the picture? God made the frogs and bugs and snails that like water, too.

PRAYER
Dear God, I'm glad You made the fish
and frogs and all the water animals.

A BIBLE VERSE TO REMEMBER

So God created the great creatures of the sea and every living and moving thing with which the water teems, according to their kinds.

GENESIS 1:21a

God Made the Birds
GENESIS 1:20–23

God said, "Let there be birds." God made big birds and little birds. Some birds have bright-colored feathers. Other birds sing pretty songs. Some birds can fly a long way, and some birds don't fly much at all.

So many different kinds of birds! And God made them all.

PRAYER
I like to watch the pretty birds, God.
They make me happy.

A BIBLE VERSE TO REMEMBER
So God created . . . every winged bird according to its kind.

GENESIS 1:21

God Made the Animals
GENESIS 1:24, 25

The world is full of animals that God made. And all of them are different.

Can you find the deer and her fawn? Can you find the bunnies and the butterfly? What other animals do you see?

PRAYER
Thank You, God, for bunnies that hop
and pretty butterflies.

A BIBLE VERSE TO REMEMBER
And God said, "Let the land produce living creatures according to their kinds."

GENESIS 1:24a

God Made Adam and Eve
GENESIS 1:26–31; 2:4–25

The world God made was a wonderful place. Then God made the first man and called him Adam.

God said, "It isn't good for Adam to be alone." So God made a woman to be Adam's wife. She was called Eve. Together they took care of the world God had made.

PRAYER
I love You, God, and the
wonderful world You made.

A BIBLE VERSE TO REMEMBER
So God created man in his own image, in the image of
God he created him; male and female he created them.

GENESIS 1:27

God's Special Day
GENESIS 2:1–3

At last God finished making the world. He looked at all He had made and said, "My world is good." Then God rested on a special day.

We remember God's special day by going to church. We pray and sing to show God how much we love Him.

PRAYER
Dear God, I love to go to church
on Your special day!

A BIBLE VERSE TO REMEMBER

I was glad when they said unto me, Let us go into the house of the Lord.

PSALM 122:1 KJV

The First Family
GENESIS 4:1, 2

Adam and Eve were the only people in the world. But soon, Adam and Eve had a baby boy. They named him Cain. "We will take good care of our son," Adam and Eve said.

After a while, they had another baby boy and named him Abel. They loved both their baby boys.

Adam and Eve and Cain and Abel were the very first family.

PRAYER
Dear God, thank You for giving
me my family to love.

A BIBLE VERSE TO REMEMBER
This is the message you heard from the beginning: We should love one another.

I JOHN 3:11

God Keeps Noah Safe
GENESIS 6:1—9:17

Look at the big boat God told Noah to build. God told Noah to take two of every kind of animal and bird into the boat. Noah did what God told him.

After Noah and his family got inside the boat, it rained and rained. God kept Noah and his family and the animals safe.

At last the rain stopped. The sun dried up the water. Noah and his family got off the ark.

God put a rainbow in the sky. He said, "When you see a rainbow, remember that I will never make a flood to cover the world again."

PRAYER
Thank You, God, for keeping me safe,
just like You kept Noah and his family safe.

A BIBLE VERSE TO REMEMBER
I will never leave you nor forsake you.

JOSHUA 1:5b

Joseph's Surprise
GENESIS 37:1–3

Joseph heard his father call him. "Come here, Joseph. I have a surprise for you."

Joseph went to his father. What do you think the surprise was? A beautiful new coat! It had many colors.

"Thank you, Father!" Joseph said. He loved his new coat. It fit just right.

Joseph knew his father loved him very much.

PRAYER
Good surprises are fun, God.
I'm glad You give me good things.

A BIBLE VERSE TO REMEMBER

Every good and perfect gift is from above, coming down
from the Father of the heavenly lights. JAMES 1:17

Miriam Helps Her Mother
EXODUS 1:22—2:10

Mother put Miriam's baby brother in a big basket. Miriam's family had to keep the baby hidden, because the Egyptian soldiers were supposed to kill Hebrew baby boys. "We'll keep you safe," she told her brother.

Miriam and her mother took the baby in his basket to the river. They put the basket in the river, and Miriam stayed to watch it.

Soon an Egyptian princess came. She saw the baby in the basket. "I will keep this baby," she said.

Miriam asked, "Should I get a Hebrew woman to take care of him?"

The princess said, "Yes." Miriam hurried home to get her mother.

"Please take care of the baby," the princess said. "I will name him Moses."

PRAYER
Please, God, help me to be a good
helper to my mother today.

28

A BIBLE VERSE TO REMEMBER
Honor your father and your mother, so that you may live
long in the land the Lord your God is giving you.

EXODUS 20:12

Moses Leads God's People
EXODUS 14

When Moses grew up, God told Moses to lead His people out of Egypt. The Egyptian king let God's people leave. But then he changed his mind and sent his soldiers after the people.

God's people were afraid. The Red Sea was in front of them. How could they get away from the soldiers?

God told Moses to hold his walking stick over the water as the people started walking. Moses obeyed God.

The wind blew, making a path in the sea. God's people walked safely across. Then Moses held his stick over the water again, and water covered the path. The soldiers couldn't reach the people.

God kept His people safe when they obeyed Him and their leader Moses.

PRAYER
Dear God, help me to obey You
and trust You when I am afraid.

A BIBLE VERSE TO REMEMBER
When I am afraid, I will trust in you.

PSALM 56:3

Ruth Finds Good Food
RUTH 2:1–23

Ruth lived with Naomi. She loved Naomi just as if Naomi were her mother. They were poor and needed food. So one day Ruth went to a farmer's field. She picked up the grain that was left after the workers cut it. She and Naomi would make bread from the grain.

Boaz, the farmer, asked, "Who is that young woman?"

"That's Ruth," Boaz's worker said.

Boaz wanted to help Ruth. He gave her lunch and told his workers to leave lots of grain for her.

When Ruth showed Naomi the grain, Naomi smiled. "God helped you find a good place to pick up grain. Now we can make the bread we need."

PRAYER
God, You are great! You know just
what I need, and You give it to me.

A BIBLE VERSE TO REMEMBER
Give thanks to the Lord, for he is good. His love endures forever.

PSALM 136:1

A New Coat for Samuel
I SAMUEL 2:18, 19

Samuel lived in God's house and helped Eli the priest. Samuel was growing. He had gotten so big that his coat was too tight and too short.

Then one day as he worked, he saw someone coming. It was his mother! Samuel was happy to see her. She had a package. What could it be? A new coat that was just the right size for Samuel!

"Thank you, Mother. You knew just what I needed," Samuel told her.

PRAYER
Thank You, God, for giving us moms
and dads who take good care of us.

A BIBLE VERSE TO REMEMBER
And my God will meet all your needs according to his glorious riches in Christ Jesus.   PHILIPPIANS 4:19

Two Good Friends
I SAMUEL 16:23; 18:1–4

David played the harp for King Saul. It made the king happy.

King Saul's son Jonathan and David became good friends. They loved each other.

Jonathan gave David his coat, sword, bow, and belt. He wanted to show how much he loved David. David and Jonathan promised to be friends as long as they lived. They even promised to be kind and loving to each other's children. And they kept their promises.

PRAYER
Dear God, help me to be a good friend to others.

A BIBLE VERSE TO REMEMBER

Love your neighbor as yourself.   MATTHEW 22:39

Elijah and the Woman Who Shared
I KINGS 17:8–16

Elijah, God's helper, was hungry and thirsty. God said, "Go to the town of Zarephath. A woman there will help you."

When Elijah found the woman, she gave him water. But she said, "I can't give you food. I only have enough for me and my little boy."

Elijah said, "Fix the food and share it with me. God will make sure you have enough."

The woman used all her oil and flour to make bread. Then God did something wonderful! She had more oil and flour!

Elijah stayed many days, and every day the woman had enough oil and flour to make more bread. Elijah said "Thank You" to God for the woman who shared her food.

PRAYER
Sometimes it's hard to share, God. Please help
me share what I have with my friends.

A BIBLE VERSE TO REMEMBER
And do not forget to do good and to share with others, for with such sacrifices God is pleased.   HEBREWS 13:16

A Girl Who Helped
II KINGS 5:1–16

The girl saw that Naaman's wife was sad. Naaman was a strong soldier, but he was very sick. The girl, who worked for Naaman's wife, said, "I know someone who can help Naaman. Elisha, one of God's helpers, will tell him how to be well."

Naaman went to see Elisha. Elisha said, "God can make you well." Naaman was told to wash in the river seven times.

Naaman did what Elisha said, and God made him well and strong. Naaman was happy. The girl was happy, too, because she could help.

PRAYER
Dear God, I want to be Your helper,
just like the girl who helped Naaman.

A BIBLE VERSE TO REMEMBER
Whenever you possibly can, do good to those who need it.

PROVERBS 3:27 TEV

Daniel Loves God
DANIEL 6

A new rule said that people should pray to the king. They would be punished for praying to God. But Daniel loved God. He kept praying to God.

The king's soldiers put Daniel in the lions' den as his punishment. All night Daniel stayed with the lions. He knew God would take care of him.

In the morning the king hurried to the lions' den. Daniel was still there. The lions didn't hurt him.

The king had Daniel pulled out of the lions' den. Then he made another rule. He told his people, "Everyone should love God."

PRAYER
Dear God, help me to love You
the way Daniel loved You.

*A BIBLE VERSE
TO REMEMBER*
*Love the Lord your
God with all your
heart and with all
your soul and with
all your mind.*

MATTHEW 22:37

Jesus Is Born
LUKE 2:1–7

Mary and Joseph finally arrived in Bethlehem. They had traveled all day, and Mary was tired. Soon her baby would be born. An angel had told Mary that the baby would be God's own Son.

The only place Mary and Joseph could find to stay was a stable—the place where animals lived.

That night, the baby was born. Mary wrapped Him in soft cloth and put Him in the manger—a box filled with hay. Mary said, "The angel told me to name Him Jesus."

PRAYER
Dear God, thank You for sending
Your Son Jesus to earth as a baby.

A BIBLE VERSE TO REMEMBER
For to us a child is born, to us a son is given. ISAIAH 9:6a

The Shepherds Learn about Jesus
LUKE 2:8–20

One night some shepherds were out in a field taking care of their sheep. An angel came to them and said, "Don't be afraid. I have wonderful news. God's Son was born today in Bethlehem. You will find Him wrapped in soft cloth and lying in a manger."

All of a sudden, many, many more angels appeared and sang a beautiful song to God.

When the angels went back to heaven, the shepherds went to Bethlehem. There they found Baby Jesus, God's Son, just as the angel told them. The shepherds went home, thanking God for what they had seen and heard. They were glad that God had sent His Son.

PRAYER
Dear Lord Jesus, I love You. I am
glad I can learn about You.

A BIBLE VERSE TO REMEMBER
Today in the town of David a Savior has been born to you;
he is Christ the Lord.   LUKE 2:11

The Wise Men Find Baby Jesus
MATTHEW 2:1–12

In a land far away from Bethlehem, some Wise Men saw a new star in the sky. One of them said, "A new star means someone special has been born. God put the star in the sky. If we follow it, we will find the baby."

The Wise Men took wonderful presents for the baby and started their long trip. They followed the star for a long time. When they got to Bethlehem, the star stopped.

"This must be where we'll find the baby," they said. They knocked on the door of a house.

When they went into the house, they saw little Jesus. How happy they were! They gave Him their presents. They bowed down and worshiped Him.

PRAYER
When I look at the stars, God, help me
remember the special star that showed
the Wise Men where Your Son was.

A BIBLE VERSE TO REMEMBER

When they saw the star, they were overjoyed.   MATTHEW 2:10

Jesus at the Temple
LUKE 2:40–52

Mary and Joseph were on their way home from Jerusalem where they had been worshiping God. They looked everywhere, but they couldn't find Jesus.

"Maybe He stayed in Jerusalem," Joseph said.

"He's only twelve. That's too young to stay without us!" His mother, Mary, said.

Mary and Joseph went back to look for Jesus. They found Him in the temple. He was asking the teachers questions and learning about God. "Jesus, we worried about You," said Mary. "But we are happy we found You safe."

"Mother," Jesus answered, "didn't you know I would be in My Father's house?"

Jesus went home with Mary and Joseph. He knew when He grew up He would tell people about His Father in heaven.

PRAYER
Dear Jesus, help me learn more and more about
You and Your Father God as I get bigger.

A BIBLE VERSE TO REMEMBER
And the child grew and became strong; he was filled with wisdom, and the grace of God was upon him. LUKE 2:40

John Tells People about Jesus
MATTHEW 3:1–6, 13–17

God had a special job for Jesus' cousin John. John was to tell people that God's Son was coming.

One day when Jesus came to John, God spoke to John. He said, "This is My dear Son. I am very pleased with Him."

Then John knew that his cousin Jesus was God's Son. He told the people, "Jesus is God's Son. Listen to what He says."

Many people believed what John said. They listened to Jesus talk about God.

PRAYER
Dear God, I want to be like John and
tell my friends about Your Son, Jesus.

A BIBLE VERSE TO REMEMBER

And a voice from heaven said, "This is my Son, whom I love;
with him I am well pleased."　　　　　　　　　MATTHEW 3:17

The Fishermen Meet Jesus
LUKE 5:1–11

Peter and Andrew were fishermen. They were sad. They hadn't caught any fish. Just then Jesus walked up to Peter and Andrew. "May I get in your boat?" He asked them.

"Yes," said Peter. And he rowed away from the shore. Jesus saw that they hadn't caught any fish. He told Peter to put their nets in the deep water.

When Peter and Andrew did what Jesus told them to, they caught so many fish their nets started to break. Peter had to call James and John, two other fishermen, to help them.

"Why did You do this?" Peter asked Jesus. "I am not good."

"I wanted to show that I love you," Jesus said. "I want you to help Me tell people about God."

So Peter, Andrew, James, and John left their boats to help Jesus.

PRAYER
Dear Jesus, I want to be Your helper, and tell people about God, just like the fishermen did.

A BIBLE VERSE TO REMEMBER

"Come, follow me," Jesus said, "and I will make you fishers of men."

MARK 1:17

Jesus Stops the Storm
MATTHEW 8:23–27

Jesus was tired. He got into a boat with His helpers. Jesus went to sleep while the boat went across the lake.

While they were in the middle of the lake, a big storm began. The wind blew and the rain pounded down. Waves splashed into the boat.

Jesus' helpers were afraid. They had never seen a storm so bad. They woke Jesus up. "Save us, Jesus. The boat is going to sink!" they cried.

"Why are you afraid?" Jesus asked. "I won't let anything happen to you."

Then Jesus stood up and said, "Wind, stop blowing." The strong wind became a gentle breeze. The waves quit splashing, and the storm stopped.

Jesus could stop the storm because He is God's Son.

PRAYER
You are wonderful, Jesus. You are stronger than the strongest storm because You are God's Son.

A BIBLE VERSE TO REMEMBER
The men were amazed and asked, "What kind of man is this?
Even the winds and the waves obey him!"　　MATTHEW 8:27

Jesus Makes a Sick Girl Well
MARK 5:22–24, 35–43

Jairus saw Jesus up the road. He hurried to talk to Jesus. "My daughter is sick, Jesus," Jairus said. "Will You come and touch her? Then she'll be well again."

Jesus knew that Jairus believed in Him. So Jesus went with Jairus to his house. But before they got in the house, a friend of Jairus's said, "Jairus, your daughter died. Even Jesus can't help her now."

Jairus was very sad. But Jesus told him, "Don't worry. I can still help her. Just believe."

Jesus went to the little girl and took her hand. "Little girl," He said, "get up."

The girl got up. She was alive. Jesus had made her well! Jairus was happy. He knew that Jesus could do anything!

PRAYER
Dear Jesus, I believe in You. I believe
You can make sick people well.

A BIBLE VERSE TO REMEMBER
Don't be afraid; just believe.

MARK 5:36b

Jesus Feeds the People
JOHN 6:1–14

One day Jesus was talking to a very large crowd. They had traveled a long way and were tired. Jesus knew they were hungry, too. They hadn't brought any food with them.

Jesus felt sorry for the people. "Let's give them something to eat," Jesus told His helpers.

"How can we get money to buy food for so many people?" Philip asked.

Andrew said, "One boy has a lunch. He has five loaves and two fish. But that isn't nearly enough for this crowd."

Jesus told His helpers, "Have the people sit on the ground." Then He took the five loaves and two fish in His hands. He said thank You to God. Jesus broke the food into pieces. His helpers gave the pieces to the people. There was enough food to feed everyone, with lots left over. Jesus used one little boy's lunch to feed lots of hungry people.

PRAYER
Dear Jesus, help me to be cheerful when
I share my things with other people.

A BIBLE VERSE TO REMEMBER
God loves a cheerful giver.   II CORINTHIANS 9:7b

Jesus Visits Mary and Martha
LUKE 10:38–42

One day Jesus went to visit His friends Mary and Martha. Mary sat down to listen to Jesus talk about God. But Martha was very busy fixing dinner.

After a while, Martha got upset because Mary wasn't helping with the work. Martha went to Jesus and said, ''Tell Mary to help me fix dinner.''

Jesus said, ''Martha, don't be upset. I'm glad you want to cook dinner for Me. And I'm glad Mary wants to listen to Me. It's important to listen to Me.''

PRAYER
Dear God, help me to listen to the
people who will teach me about You.

A BIBLE VERSE TO REMEMBER

Listen, my son, to your father's instruction and do not forsake your mother's teaching.

PROVERBS 1:8

Jesus and the Children
MARK 10:13–16

Jesus was teaching people about His Father God. Some people were bringing their children to Jesus.

Jesus' helpers said, "No. Jesus doesn't have time to see your children."

But Jesus heard His helpers. He said, "Let the little children come to Me. Don't stop them."

The children ran to Jesus and hugged Him. He held them and blessed them.

PRAYER
I'm so happy You love children,
Jesus. I love You, too.

A BIBLE VERSE TO REMEMBER

Let the little children come to me, and do not hinder them,
for the kingdom of God belongs to such as these. MARK 10:14b

Jesus Helps Bartimaeus
MARK 10:46–52

Bartimaeus sat beside the road. He was sad because he was blind. He couldn't see the people or donkeys that went by. One day he heard a loud crowd going by. "What is happening?" he called.

"Jesus is coming," someone said.

"Jesus, Jesus!" Bartimaeus called. "Please help me."

Jesus stopped and called for Bartimaeus to come to Him. "What do you want?" Jesus asked kindly.

"Master, I want to see," Bartimaeus answered.

"You are well. I'm glad you believe I can help you." Jesus said.

Bartimaeus looked around. He could see Jesus and the people and the donkeys! Jesus had made him well. "Thank You, Jesus," Bartimaeus exclaimed, and he followed Jesus down the road.

PRAYER
Dear Jesus, I'm so glad You love to
help people. Please help me today.

A BIBLE VERSE TO REMEMBER
My help comes from the Lord, the Maker of heaven and earth.

PSALM 121:2

The People Welcome Jesus
MARK 11:1–11

Go into the village," Jesus told His helpers. "You'll see a donkey. Bring it to Me. If someone asks what you are doing, tell them I need it."

The helpers brought the donkey to Jesus. They put their coats on its back. Jesus rode the donkey as they went into Jerusalem.

As they got near the city, people saw them. "Jesus is coming!" they said. They were so happy they made a path for Him with their coats and palm branches. "Hosanna!" they shouted, to tell Jesus how happy they were and how much they loved Him. They knew Jesus was special. He told them wonderful things about God.

Jesus smiled at the people. He was glad they wanted to learn about God.

PRAYER
*I will shout "Hosanna!" too, Jesus,
because I love You so much.*

A BIBLE VERSE TO REMEMBER
Hosanna! Blessed is he who comes in the name of the Lord!

MARK 11:9b

Jesus Lives!
MATTHEW 28:1–10; LUKE 23:44—24:12; JOHN 20:1–10

Jesus' friends were sad. Men had killed Jesus. His friends buried His body in a cave called a tomb.

Early one morning some women went to the tomb. They wanted to put sweet-smelling spices on Jesus' body.

When they got to the tomb, the heavy stone that had been in front of the tomb was rolled away from the door. The women hurried inside. They saw two shining angels, but no Jesus.

"Why are you looking here for Jesus?" the angels asked. "He isn't dead anymore. He is alive again, just as He said He would be."

The women were excited! They ran to tell Jesus' helpers. Peter and John ran to the tomb and looked in. All they saw were the sheets that had been around His body.

Jesus wasn't dead! He was alive again!

PRAYER
Dear Jesus, I am so glad You are alive!

A BIBLE VERSE TO REMEMBER

He is not here; he has risen, just as he said. Come and see the place where he lay.

MATTHEW 28:6

Dorcas Helps People
ACTS 9:36–43

Dorcas loved to help people. She made clothes and gave them to poor people.

One day Dorcas got sick and died. The people she had helped were sad. They missed Dorcas. Some of her friends sent for Peter, one of Jesus' helpers.

The people showed Peter the clothes Dorcas had made. Peter went into Dorcas's room. He asked the people to leave.

Peter prayed to God. Then he turned to Dorcas. "Get up, Dorcas," he said.

Dorcas opened her eyes and saw Peter. She sat up. Peter helped her get up and took her out to see her friends.

Everyone was happy. They were glad God let Dorcas live again. They told other people what God had done, and more people believed in God.

PRAYER
Thank You, God, for people like Dorcas.
I want to help people, too.

A BIBLE VERSE TO REMEMBER

Command them to do good, to be rich in good deeds, and to be generous and willing to share.
I TIMOTHY 6:18

Peter Meets Cornelius
ACTS 10

Peter was staying at a friend's house. While he was waiting for lunch, he went up on the flat roof to pray to God.

God showed Peter that He loves all different kinds of people.

God sent three men to the house where Peter was staying. They asked him to go with them to see a man named Cornelius. Cornelius was from another country. But Peter knew God loved people in all countries, so he went with them to Cornelius's house.

Cornelius invited his friends and family to hear Peter. Cornelius loved God, but he didn't know about Jesus. Peter told all of the people that Jesus loved them. They were thankful Peter had come to tell them about Jesus. They learned to love God.

PRAYER
You love people everywhere, God.
I am glad someone told me about You.

A BIBLE VERSE TO REMEMBER

Therefore go and make disciples of all nations, baptizing them in the name of the Father and of the Son and of the Holy Spirit.

MATTHEW 28:19

Timothy Learns about God
ACTS 16:1–5; II Timothy 1:1–8; 3:14–17

Timothy liked to listen to his mother and grandmother tell stories. They told him about God.

Timothy's mother and grandmother loved God. They taught Timothy to pray. They wanted him to grow up loving God, too.

When Timothy grew up, he helped his friend Paul tell other people about God and Jesus. Paul loved Timothy just as if Timothy were his own son. Paul told him, "Tell everyone about Jesus, as I do. Don't be afraid to tell them."

Timothy remembered what his mother and grandmother taught him. He prayed to God for help, and he did what Paul wanted him to do.

PRAYER
Dear God, help me to love You now and when I
grow up. I want You to be my friend always.

*A BIBLE VERSE
TO REMEMBER
And you remember
that ever since you
were a child, you
have known the Holy
Scriptures, which are
able to give you the
wisdom that leads to
salvation through
faith in Christ Jesus.*

II TIMOTHY 3:15 TEV

God Takes Care of Paul and Silas
ACTS 16:16–34

Wherever they went, Paul and Silas told people about God. They loved God and wanted other people to love Him, too.

In one city, some men didn't like what Paul and Silas were saying. They put Paul and Silas in jail.

Paul and Silas knew God still loved them. So they sang songs and prayed, even in the middle of the night. They knew God could hear them.

Suddenly there was an earthquake. The ground shook so hard the jail doors flew open.

The jail keeper was afraid. But Paul called to him, ''Don't worry. We're still here.''

The jail keeper knew God loved Paul and Silas and took care of them. He wanted God to take care of him, too. He took Paul and Silas to his house and listened as they told him about Jesus and God. The jail keeper and his family trusted God.

PRAYER
Dear God, help me to pray and sing to
You even when I'm having hard times.

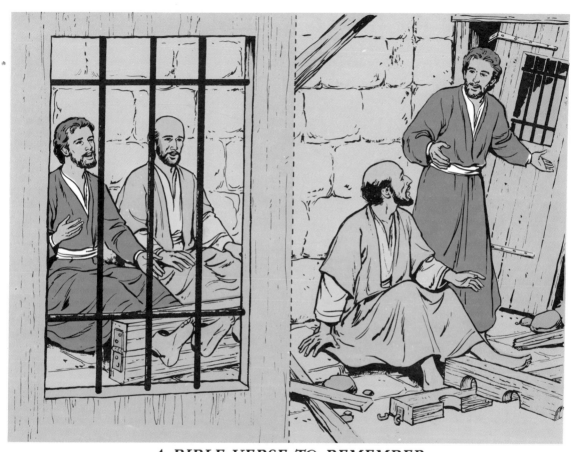

A BIBLE VERSE TO REMEMBER
Speak to one another with psalms, hymns, and spiritual songs. Sing and make music in your heart to the Lord.

EPHESIANS 5:19